Maynard

Success Coloring Book

Tamara Fox

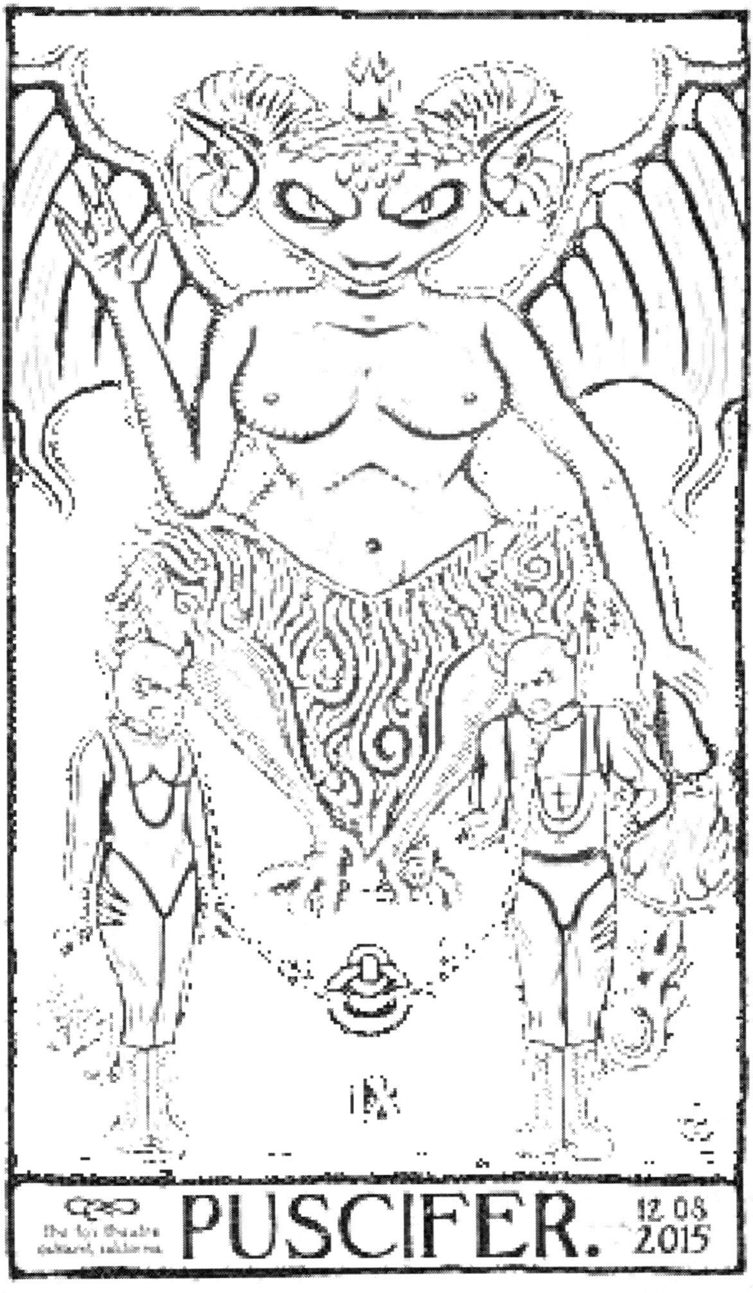
PUSCIFER.
12.08
2015

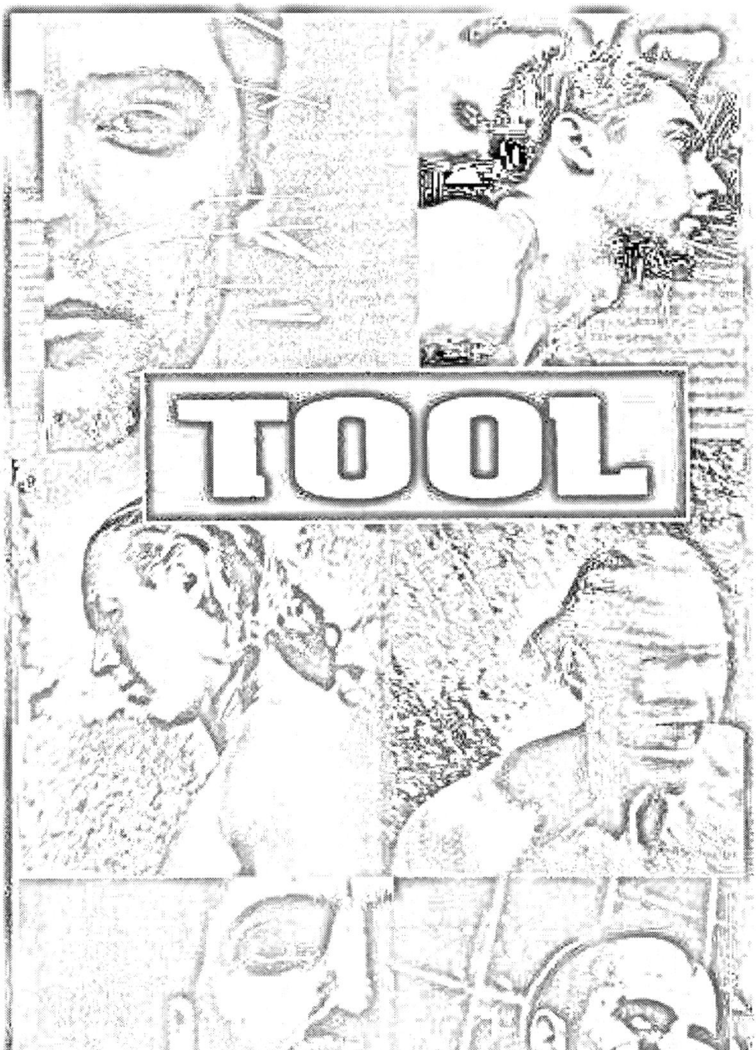
TOOL

TOOL
SELLAND ARENA • MARCH 14TH 2014 • FRESNO, CA

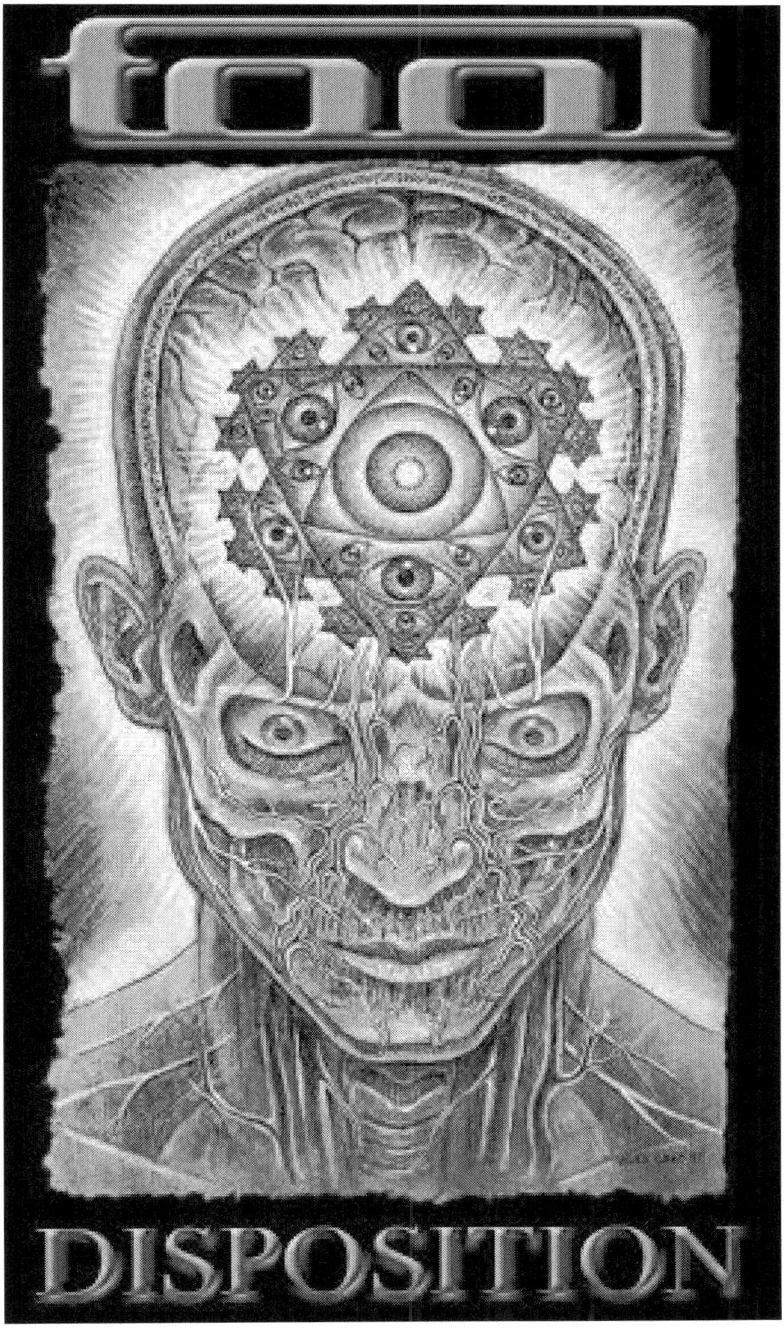
tool
DISPOSITION

TOOL
25 JUNI 2001 · MONTAG · 21 Uhr
COLUMBIAHALLE
BERLIN

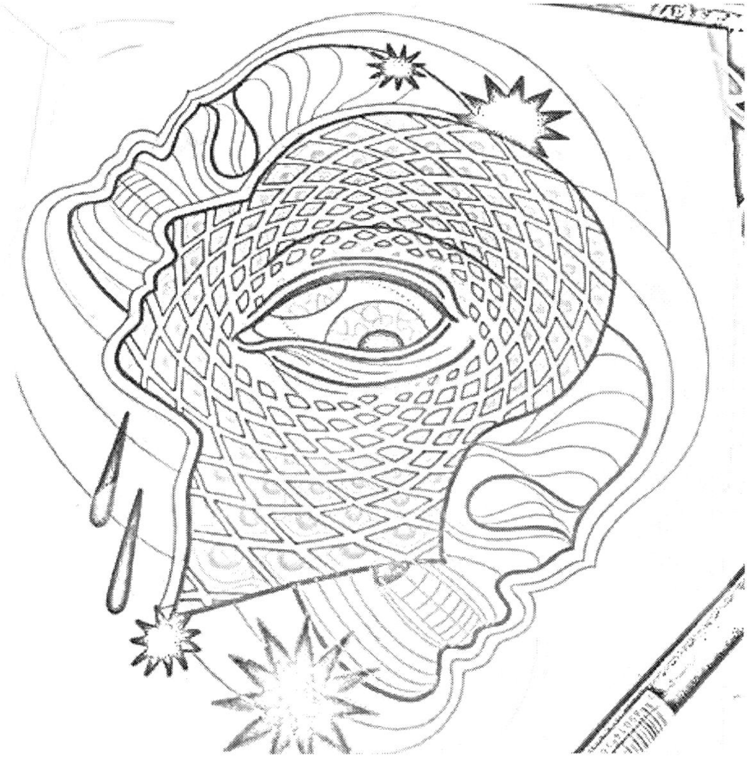

PUSCIFER
LOS ANGELES

TOOL
WITH SPECIAL GUEST
MESHUGGAH
SUNDAY, OCTOBER 13TH
COLORADO SPRINGS WORLD ARENA

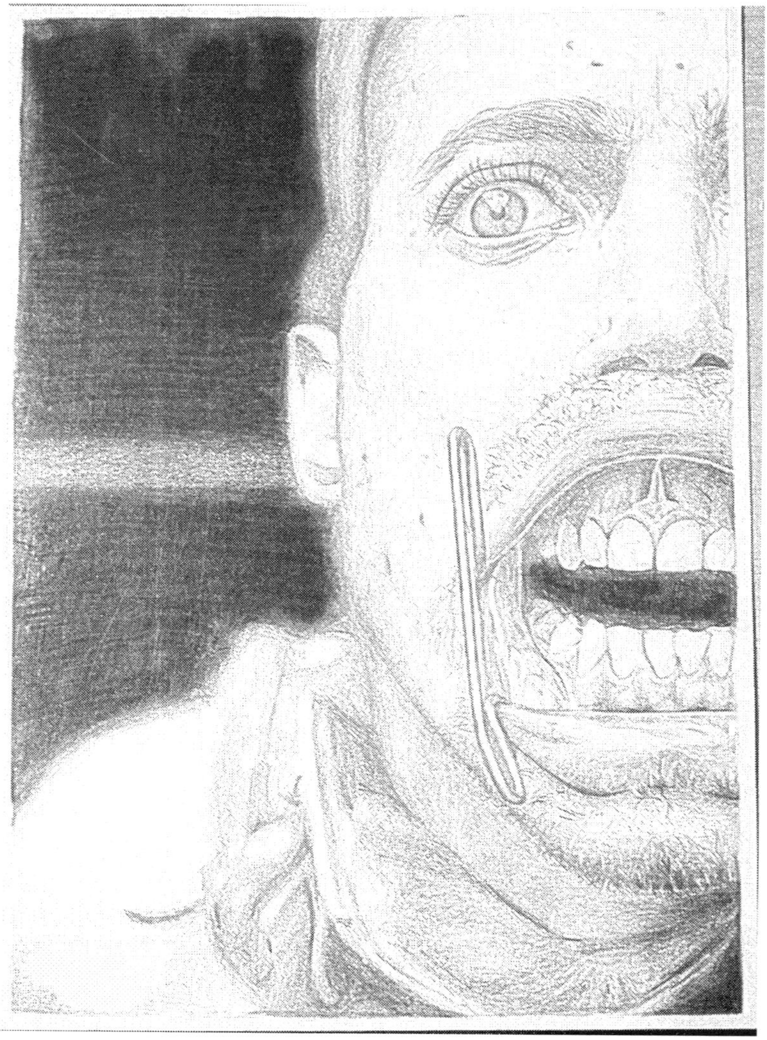

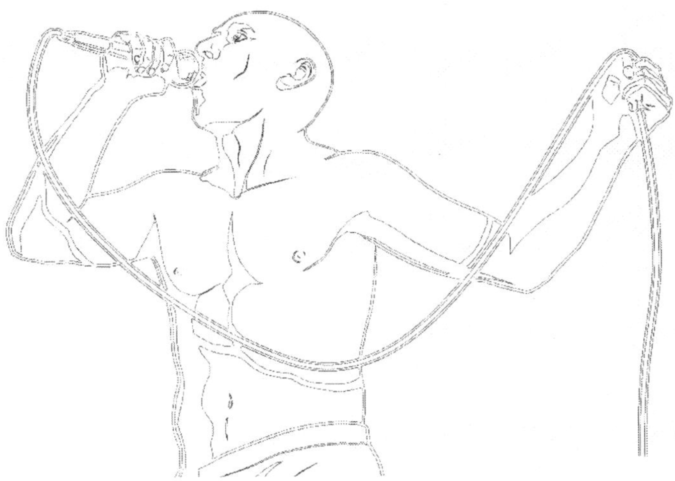

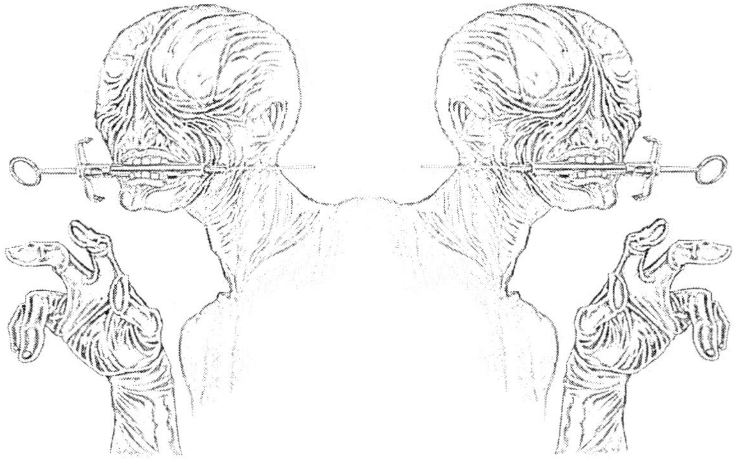

tool
WITH SPECIAL GUESTS
SIDNEY MYER MUSIC BOWL WED 31 JANUARY 2007

Dead
Pegasus

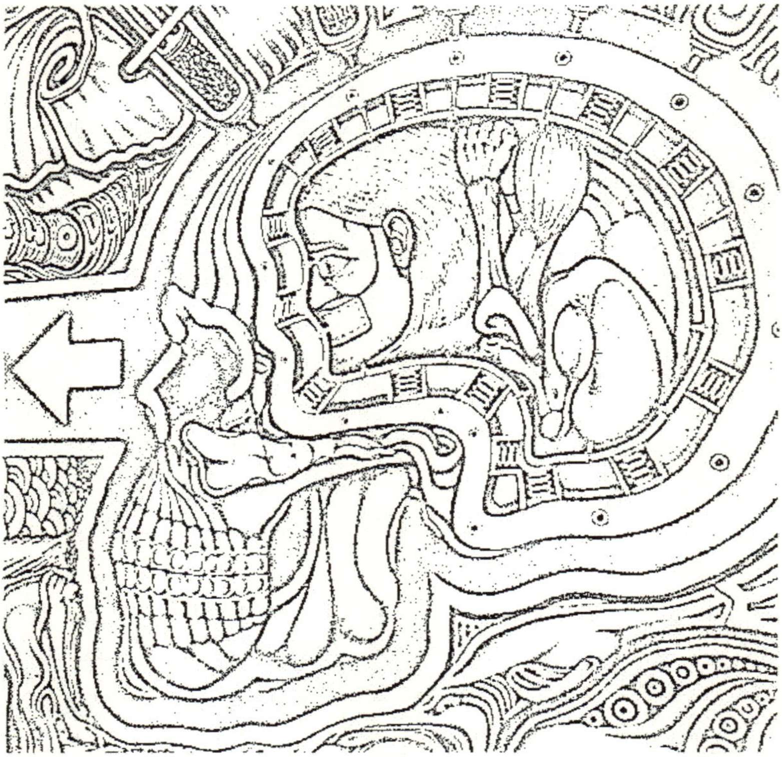

Made in the USA
Middletown, DE
16 April 2020

89145687R00021